Unusual Traditions

John McIlwain

Contents

Collins

What is a tradition?

A tradition is something which people have done in the same way for a long time. It may be a big event, like a carnival, or something small which a family does each year. In this book are some of the world's most unusual traditions.

2

Dancing traditions

The Haka – New Zealand

Members of the New Zealand All Blacks rugby team perform a traditional war dance called the Haka before every match they play. They stare at the other team with wide eyes, stamp their feet, shake their fists angrily and roar out a war chant.

The Haka is a traditional Maori dance. Maoris are from New Zealand.

The Haka war chant:
Ka mate (say *car-matty*)
Ka mate
Ka ora
Ka ora
(which means, roughly,
"It is death, it is life.")

5

Morris dancing – England

In the English countryside in summer, you may see Morris dancers – a group of people dressed in white shirts, with flowers round their hats and bells round their legs. As they dance, they knock sticks together and wave handkerchiefs. The tradition of Morris dancing is over 400 years old.

Night traditions

Flaming tar barrels – Devon, England

Each Bonfire Night, 5 November, people carry burning barrels through the streets of Ottery St Mary. They fill a barrel with rags and tar, light it, lift it onto their shoulders, and run. When it becomes too hot, they pass it on. The last person throws the barrel to the ground, and flames burst out all over the place.

The flames are dangerous, and people wear protective gloves so that they won't get burnt.

Never play with fire!

8

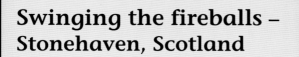

Swinging the fireballs – Stonehaven, Scotland

At midnight on New Year's Eve, men in Stonehaven burn the old year away with fireballs.

They set fire to baskets and whirl them around and around through the streets. Everyone stands well back!

 Never play with fire!

9

Animal traditions

Groundhog Day – Punxsutawney, Pennsylvania, USA

One American town keeps a special groundhog called Phil to forecast the weather! On Groundhog Day, 2 February, thousands of people wait to see Phil come out of his burrow. Tradition says that if he casts a shadow, there will be rain and snow for six more weeks. If there's no shadow, the weather will be good.

Wild groundhogs eat juicy green plants, but Phil eats dog food and ice cream!

Candlemas

Groundhog Day used to be called Candlemas. An old rhyme says:

If Candlemas Day be fair and bright,
Come, Winter, have another flight.
If Candlemas brings cloud and rain,
Go, Winter, and come not again.

Jaipur elephant festival – India

Elephants are important to people in India. Indian princes used to ride on them and they are still used for carrying things and pulling logs in the forests.

The elephant festival starts with a parade of elephants and the favourite event is the tug of war.

Paint, jewels and velvet cloth are used to make the elephants look beautiful.

Spring and summer carnivals

Spring carnival – Trinidad and Tobago

Carnivals are held in many countries around the world. In Trinidad and Tobago people prepare costumes and practise for weeks before the day of the carnival in April. On the day itself there is a huge parade of carnival floats and people in colourful outfits.

Children practise for weeks to learn difficult skills.

Everyone has fun on the big day.

Summer carnival – Rio de Janeiro, Brazil

The biggest carnival in the world is held in Rio de Janeiro.

The Rio carnival is a wonderful sight.

Winter festivals

Snow festival – Sapporo, Japan

Every winter, the people of Sapporo hold a snow festival. In Odori Park, artists carve statues from snow and ice – huge snowmen, giant castles, dolls and all kinds of wonderful things!

There are snow slides for children to whizz down.

Street carnivals – Somerset, England

Hundreds of people in Somerset work hard all year to get ready for the winter carnival season. The carnival visits each big town. Bands play, people dance and amazing floats go slowly by. These make a wonderful sight, with people in colourful costumes lit by thousands of lights.

Sports and games

Dragon boat racing – China

Dragons aren't real, but people in China believe dragons have great power over your life. They think that dragons bring luck, money and good health, and that they control the weather. People build racing boats and carve them to look like dragons.

Dragon boats need lots of people to row them.

Cheese rolling – Cotswold hills, England

When cheeses are first made they are large and round. One tradition in the Cotswolds is to roll a cheese down a steep, grassy hill and then run after it. The first person to reach the bottom is the winner.

Cheese rolling can be dangerous if the contestants run too fast!

⚠ **This is dangerous!**

Human towers – Barcelona, Spain

Each summer in Barcelona teams of people try to make the biggest human towers by standing on each other's shoulders. Some towers are nine layers high and take 170 people to make them!

Index

Traditions around the world

USA
Groundhog Day

Scotland
Swinging the fireballs

**Trinidad
and Tobago**
Spring
carnival

Spain
Human
towers

Brazil
Rio de Janeiro
Summer carnival

China
Dragon boat racing

Japan
Snow festival

New Zealand
The Haka

England
Morris dancing
Cheese rolling
Flaming tar barrels
Street carnivals

India
Jaipur elephant festival

Getting creative

- If your child's enjoyed reading about unusual traditions, they could try finding out about some others, e.g. new year celebrations around the world, or a local tradition.
- They could start by searching for information on the internet, or at the library.
- They could collect information into a poster or powerpoint-style presentation. This will help children to read for meaning and organise the information they find.
- They could design an advert for a local tradition.

Other books at Level 3:

Fiction	Non-fiction
Twinkle, Twinkle Firefly	What's that Building?
Chewy Hughie	How to be a Knight in 10 easy stages
Mountain Mona	Unusual Traditions